THE BUSKER JAZZ 'N' BLUES

ALEXANDER'S RAGTIME BAND	6
BILL BAILEY WON'T YOU PLEASE COME HOME	8
THE BIRTH OF THE BLUES	10
BLACK BOTTOM	12
CHARLESTON	14
CHEROKEE	16
CHICAGO	18
CRAZY RHYTHM	20
THE DARKTOWN STRUTTERS' BALL	22
THE ENTERTAINER	32
HE'S GOT THE WHOLE WORLD IN HIS HANDS	24
I GOT RHYTHM	26
I'M GONNA SIT RIGHT DOWN AND WRITE MYSELF A LETTER	28
IN THE MOOD	30
LIMEHOUSE BLUES	33
SKYLINER	34
SWEET GEORGIA BROWN	36
TIGER RAG	38
12TH STREET RAG	40
WHEN THE SAINTS GO MARCHING IN	43

Edited by PETER FOSS
Arranged by GARY LERNER

First Published 1989
This edition published 1994

EDUCATION DIVISION

IMP

© **International Music Publications Limited**
Southend Road, Woodford Green, Essex IG8 8HN, England

Reproducing this music in any form is illegal and forbidden
by the Copyright, Designs and Patents Act 1988

FINGERING CHART
Recorder

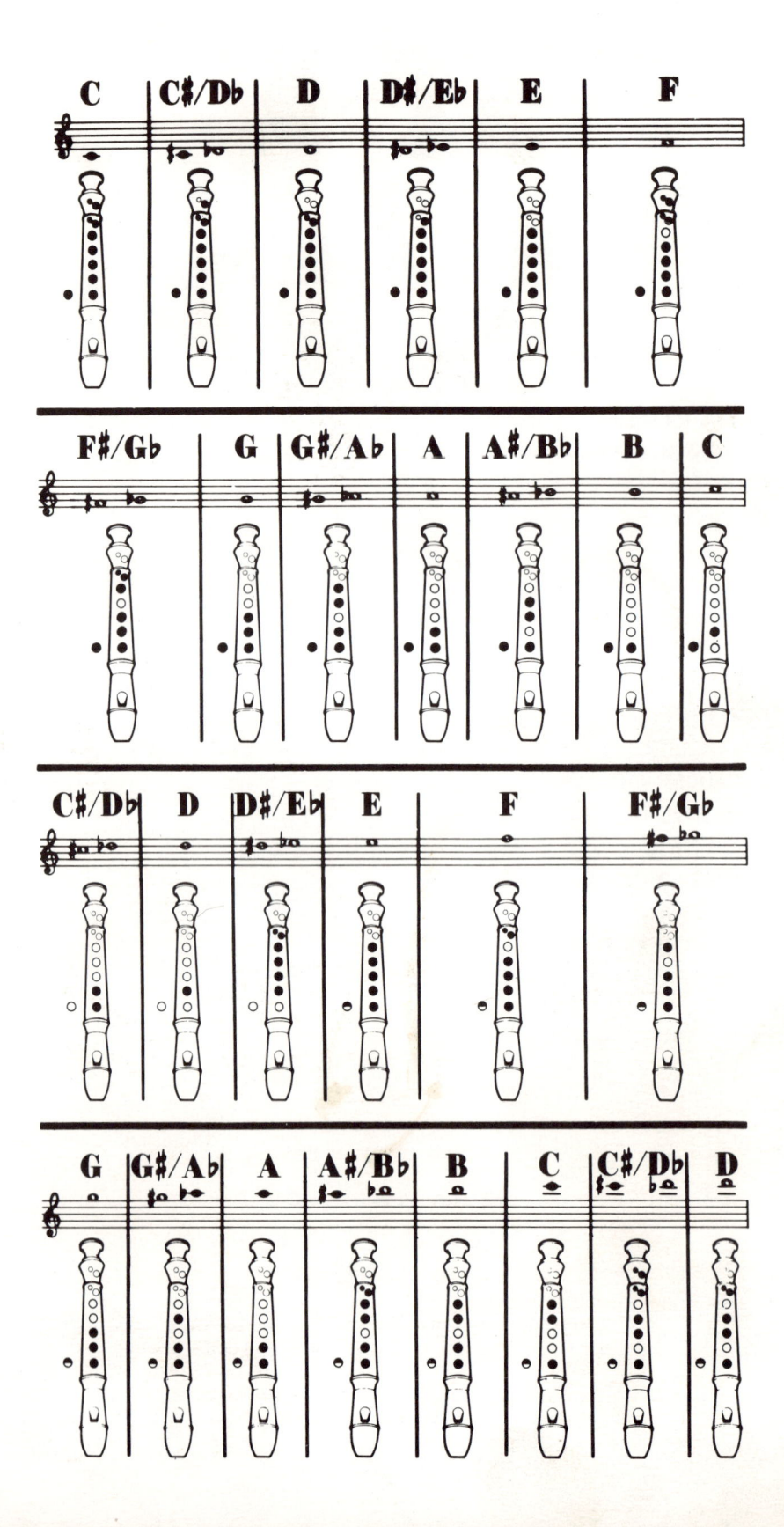

CHORD DIRECTORY
Guitar

'x' over a string means this string should not be played

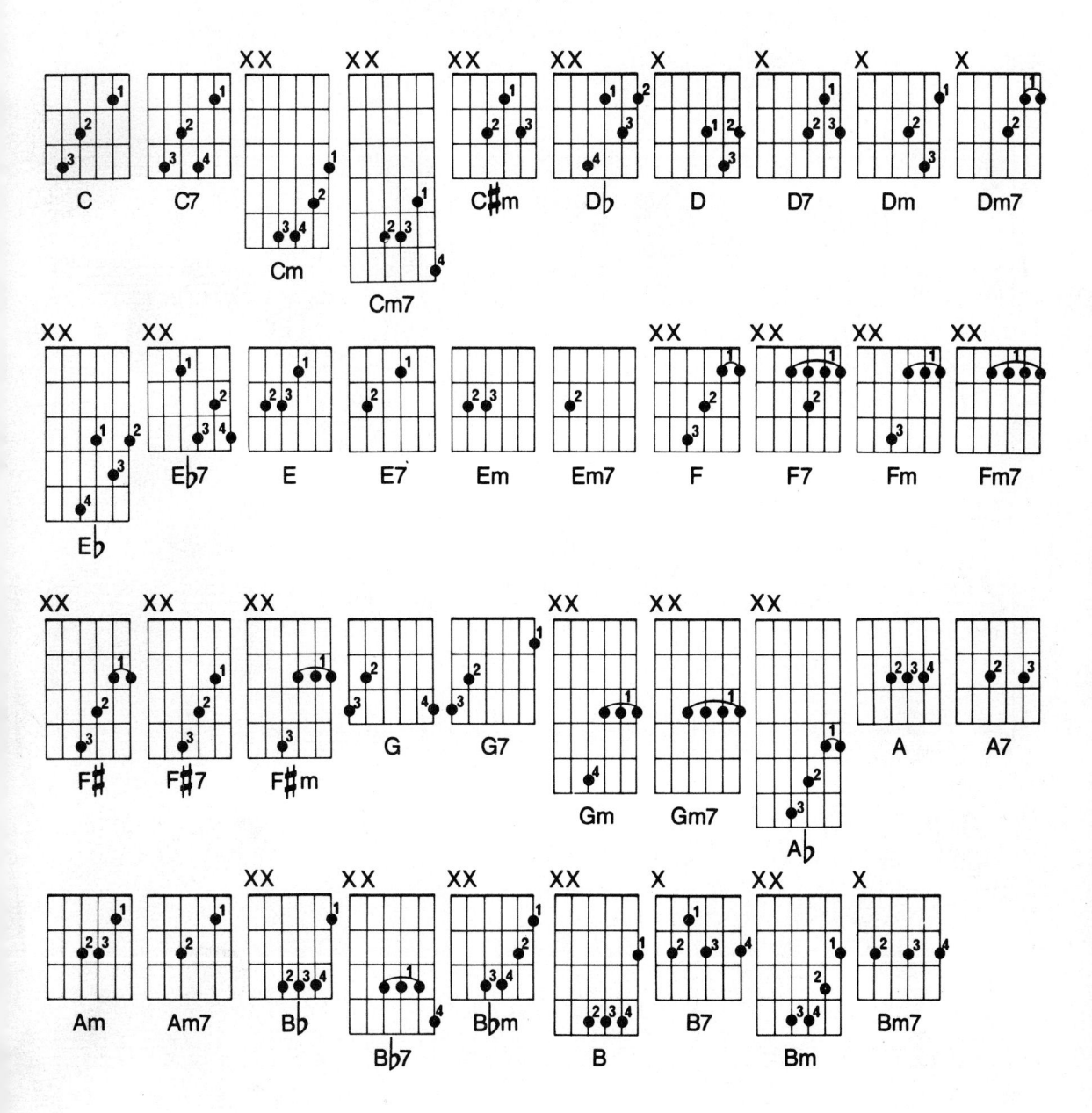

C C7 Cm Cm7 C#m Db D D7 Dm Dm7

Eb Eb7 E E7 Em Em7 F F7 Fm Fm7

F# F#7 F#m G G7 Gm Gm7 Ab A A7

Am Am7 Bb Bb7 Bbm B B7 Bm Bm7

Always make sure that your guitar is in tune with the other instruments before you start to play with other musicians.

CHORD SYMBOL GUIDE
Keyboards

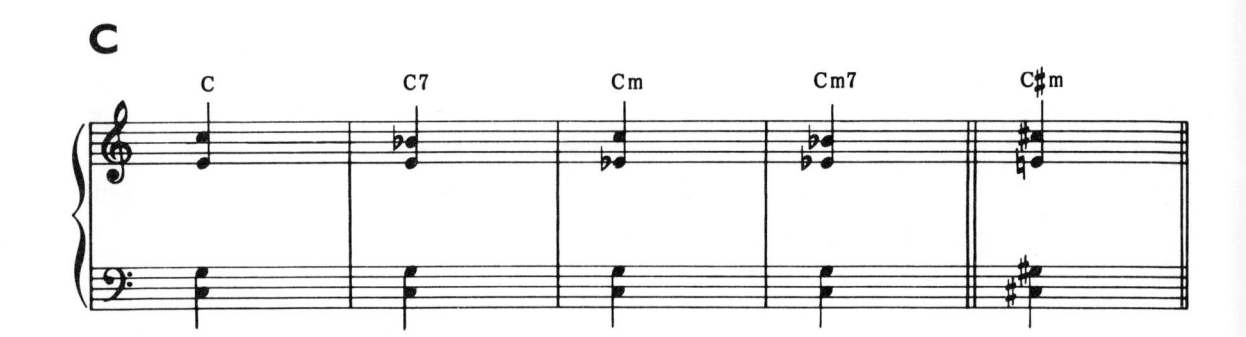

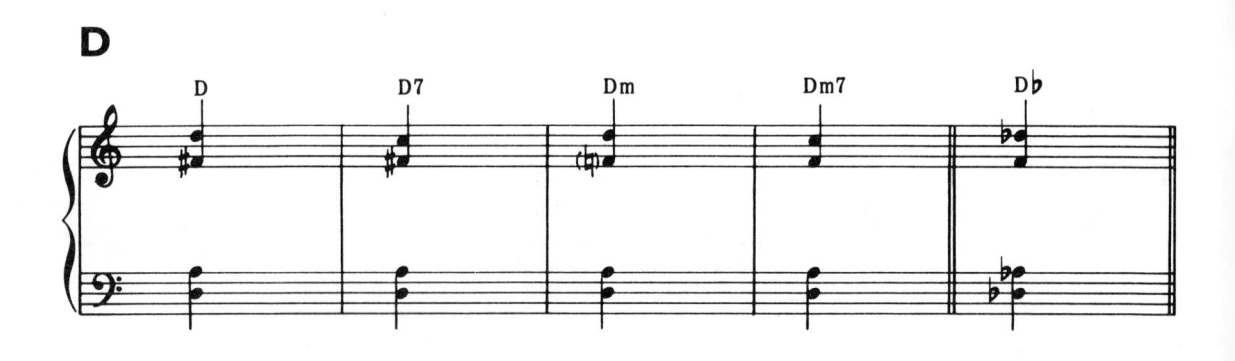

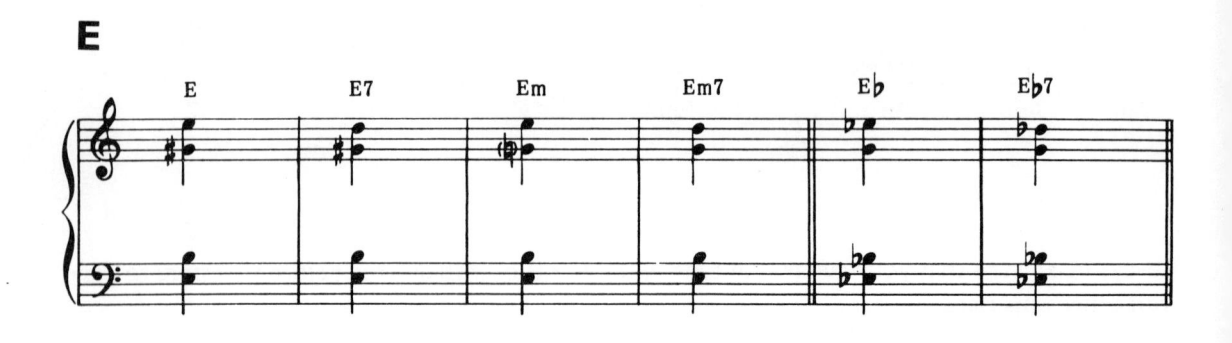

F

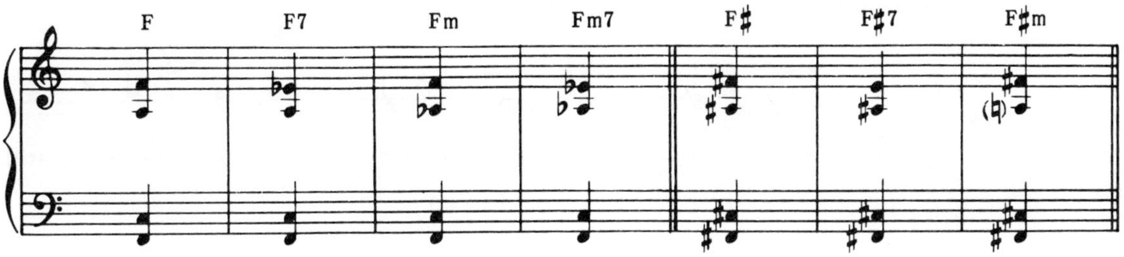

G

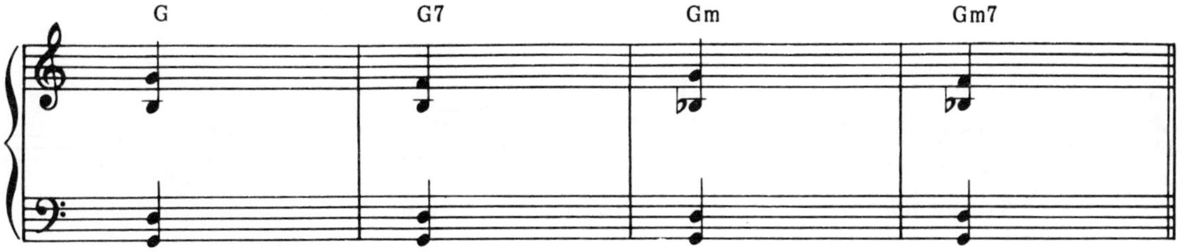

A

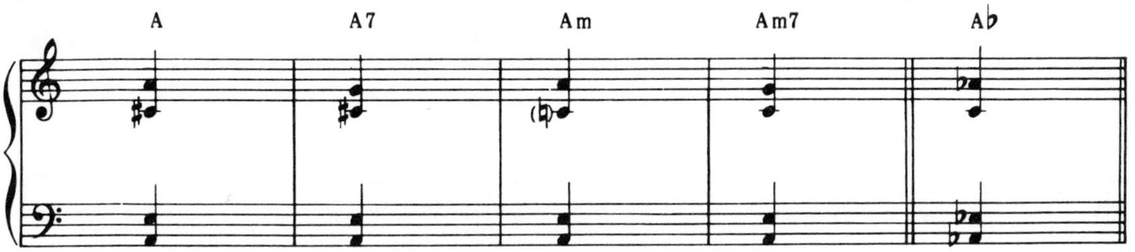

B

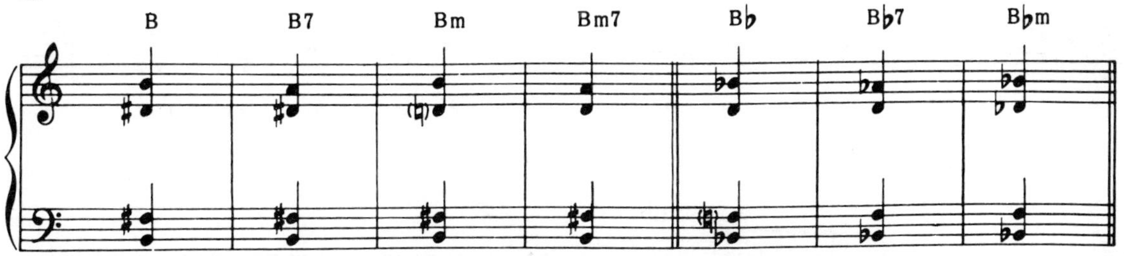

ALEXANDER'S RAGTIME BAND

Words and Music by
IRVING BERLIN

Moderately

Oh, ma hon-ey, Oh, ma hon-ey, Bet-ter hur-ry and let's me-an-der, Ain't you go-in', Ain't you go-in' To the lead-er man, rag-ged met-er man? Oh, ma hon-ey, Oh, ma hon-ey, Let me take you to Al-ex-an-der's grand stand, brass band, Ain't you com-in' a-long? Come on and hear, —— Come on and hear Al-ex-an-der's rag-time band. —— Come on and hear, —— Come on and hear, It's the

© 1911 Irving Berlin Inc., USA
B Feldman & Co. Ltd., London WC2H 0EA

best band in the land. They can play a bu-gle call like you nev-er heard be-fore, So nat-ur-al that you want to go to war; That's just the best-est band what am, hon-ey lamb. Come on a-long, —— Come on a-long, Let me take you by the hand —— Up to the man, —— Up to the man who's the lead-er of the band. —— And if you care to hear the Swan-ee Riv-er played, in rag-time, —— Come on and hear, —— Come on and hear —— Al-ex-an-der's rag-time band. Come on and band.

BILL BAILEY, WON'T YOU PLEASE COME HOME

Words and Music by
HUGHIE CANNON

Relaxed tempo

1. On one sum-mer's day the sun was shin-ing fine. The la-dy love of old Bill Bail-ey was hang-ing clothes on the line in her back yard, And cry-ing hard. 2. She wed a B. 'N O brake-man that went and threw her down, Hol-ler-ing like a prune-fed calf with a big gang hang-ing 'round and to that crowd she'd yell out loud: Won't you come home, Bill Bail-ey,

© 1989 International Music Publications Limited, Woodford Green, Essex IG8 8HN

won't you come home? She moans the whole day long. Baby I'll do the cooking, darling I'll pay the rent. I know I've done you wrong. Come on, honey, 'member that rainy evening I drove you out with nothing but a fine tooth comb. I know I'm to blame, well ain't that a shame? Bill Bailey won't you please come home?

THE BIRTH OF THE BLUES

Words and Music by
DE SYLVA, BROWN and HENDERSON

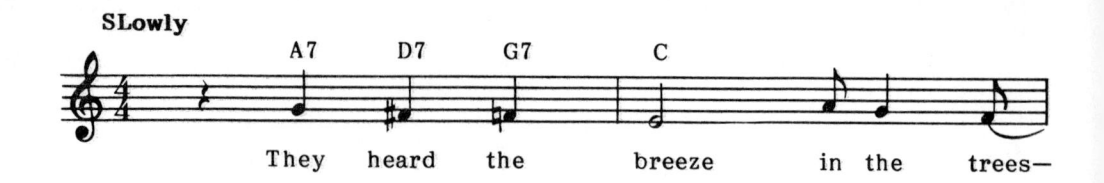

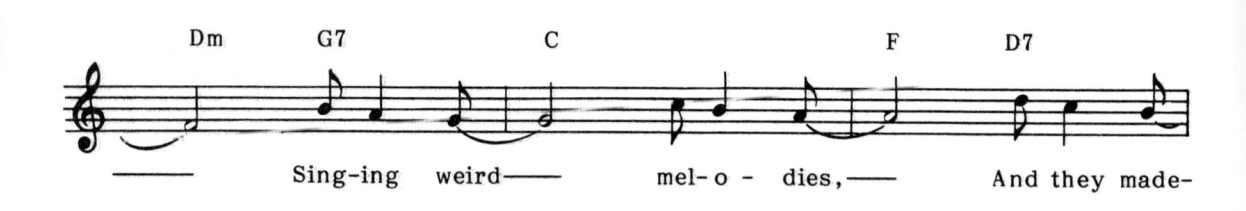

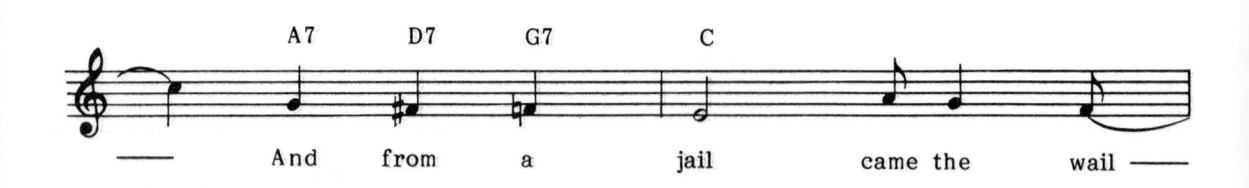

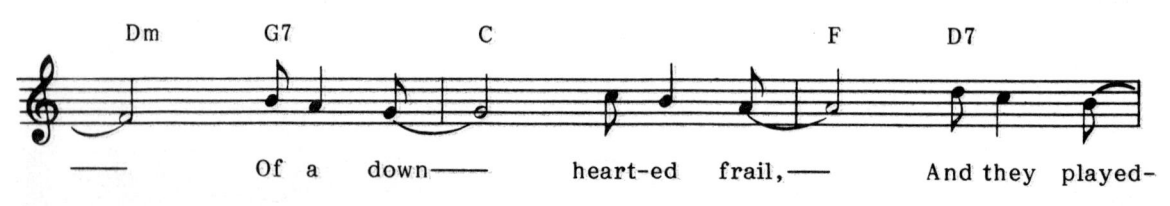

Slowly

They heard the breeze in the trees—
Sing-ing weird— mel-o-dies,— And they made—
— that — The start— of the Blues.—
— And from a jail came the wail —
— Of a down— heart-ed frail,— And they played—

© 1926 & 1989 Harms Inc., USA
Warner Chappell Music Ltd., London W1Y 3FA/Redwood Music Ltd., London NW1 8BD

— that As part of the Blues.

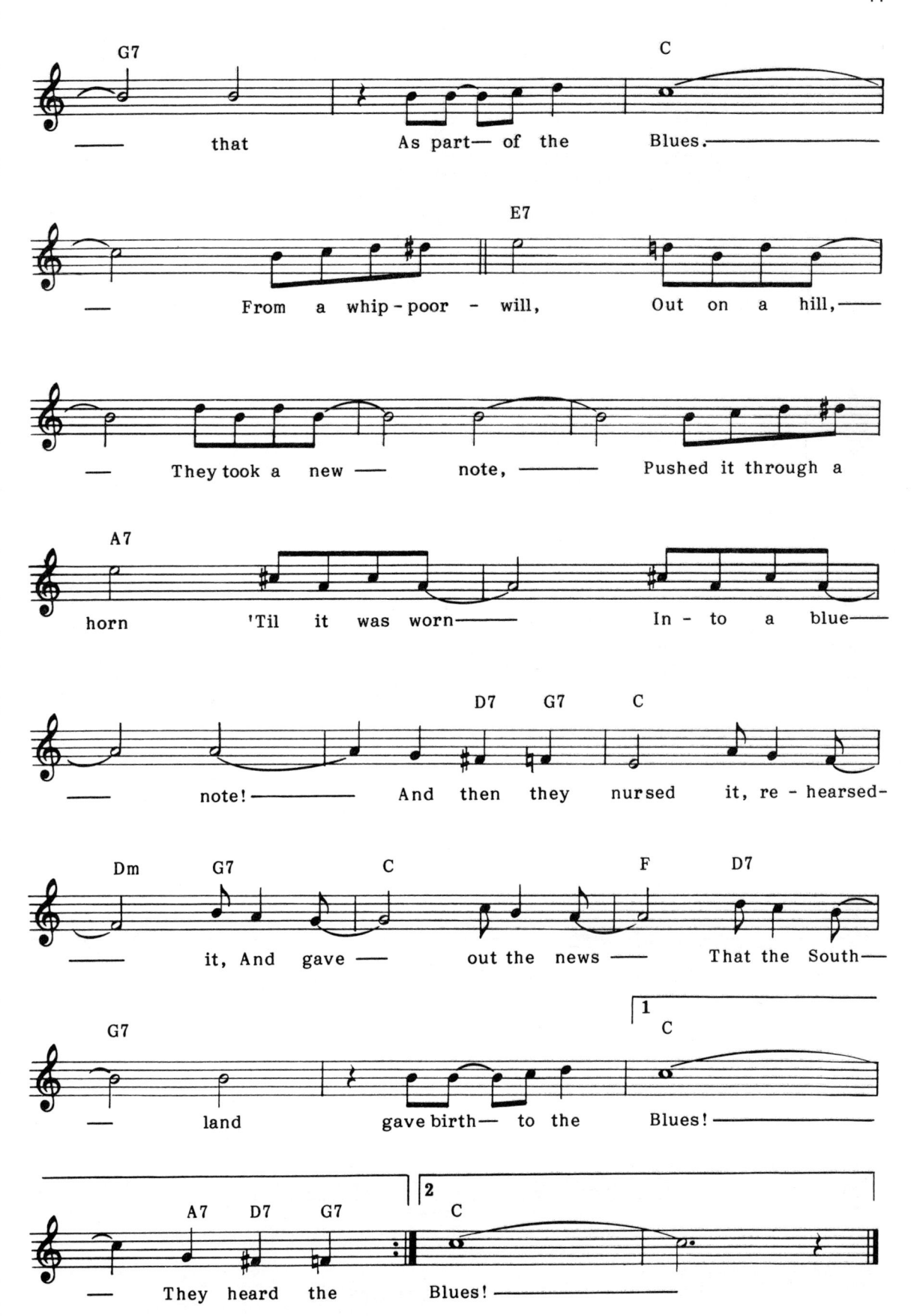

From a whip-poor-will, Out on a hill,

They took a new note, Pushed it through a

horn 'Til it was worn In to a blue

note! And then they nursed it, re-hearsed-

it, And gave out the news That the South—

1. land gave birth to the Blues!

2. They heard the Blues!

BLACK BOTTOM

Words and Music by
DE SYLVA, BROWN and HENDERSON

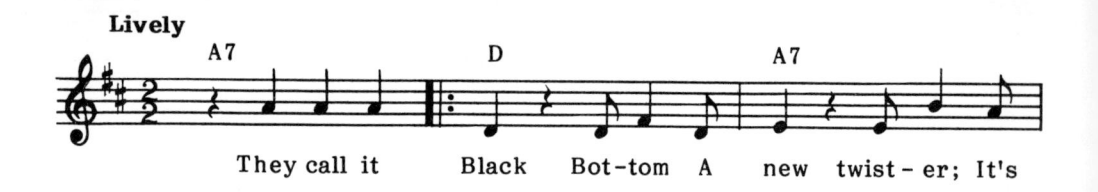

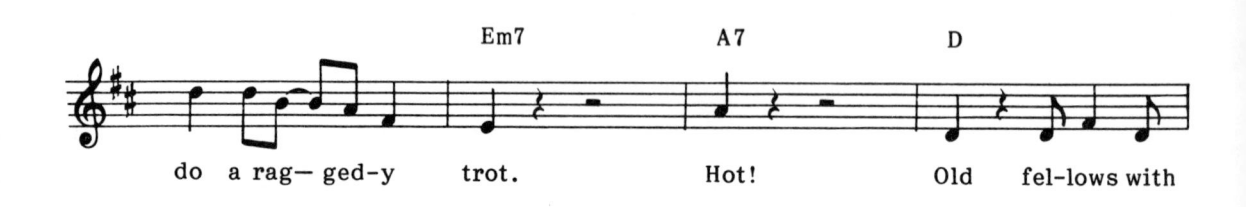

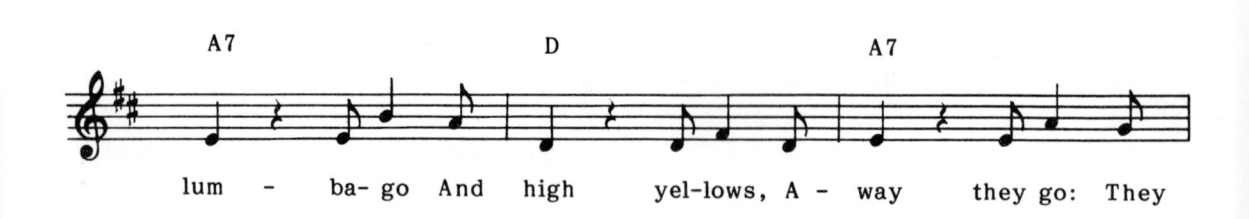

Lively

They call it Black Bot-tom A new twist-er; It's sure got 'em, And oh, Sis-ter: they clap their hands and do a rag-ged-y trot. Hot! Old fel-lows with lum-ba-go And high yel-lows, A-way they go: They jump right in and give it all— that they've got!

© 1926 & 1989 Harms Inc., USA
Warner Chappell Music Ltd., London W1Y 3FA/Redwood Music Ltd., London NW1 8BD

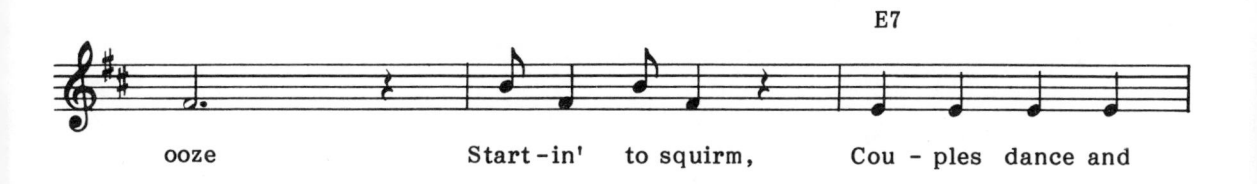

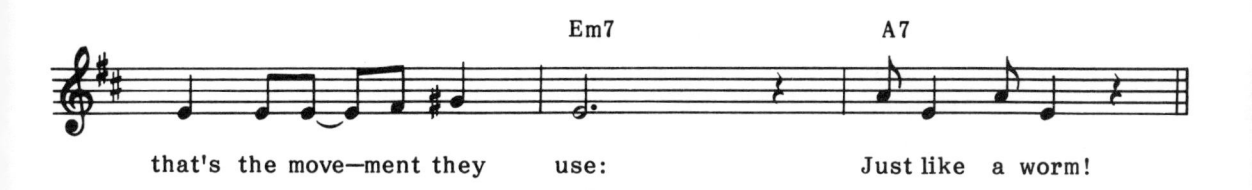

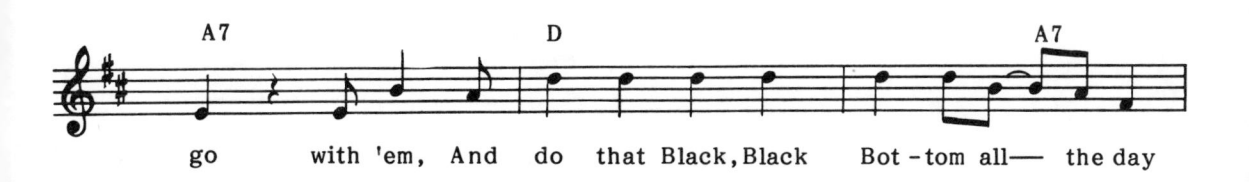

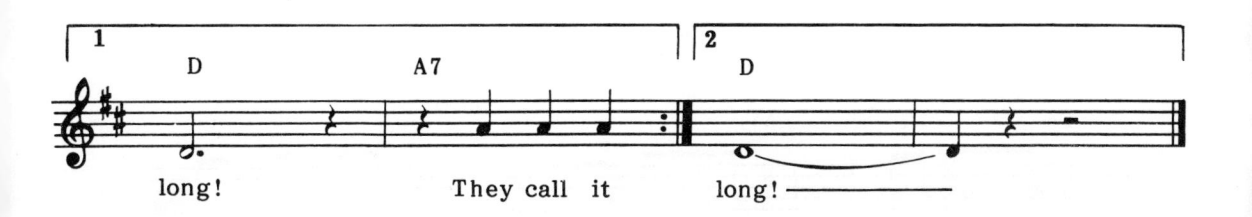

They say that when that riv-er bot-tom cov-ered with ooze Start-in' to squirm, Cou-ples dance and that's the move-ment they use: Just like a worm! Black Bot-tom, A new rhy-thm, when you spot 'em, You go with 'em, And do that Black, Black Bot-tom all— the day long! They call it long!

CHARLESTON

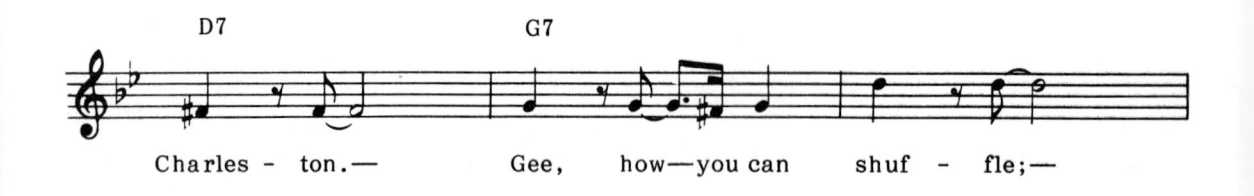

Words and Music by
CECIL MACK and JIMMY JOHNSON

Rhythmic and bright

Charles - ton! — Charles - ton! — Made in — Car - o - lin - a! — Some dance, — Some prance, — I'll say, — There's no-thing fin— er than the Charles - ton, — Charles - ton. — Gee, how— you can shuf - fle; — Ev-'ry step— you do, Leads to some— thing new. Man, I'm tell— ing you,

© 1923 & 1989 Harms Inc., USA
Warner Chappell Music Ltd., London W1Y 3FA

It's a la— pa-zoo! Buck dance,— Wing dance— Will be— a back num-ber;— But the Charles-ton,— the new Charles-ton,— That dance— is sure-ly a com— er.

Some - time— You'll— dance it one time,— That— dance called Charles-ton,— Made in South—Car-o -

1. line!—

2. line!—

CHEROKEE

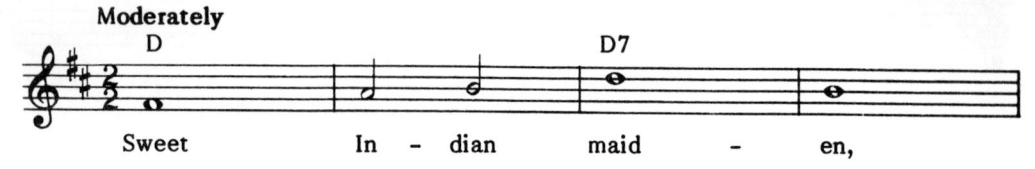

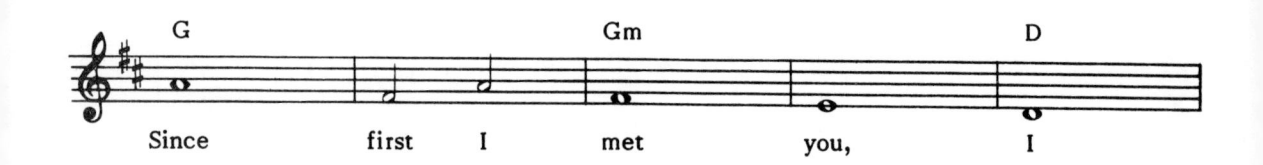

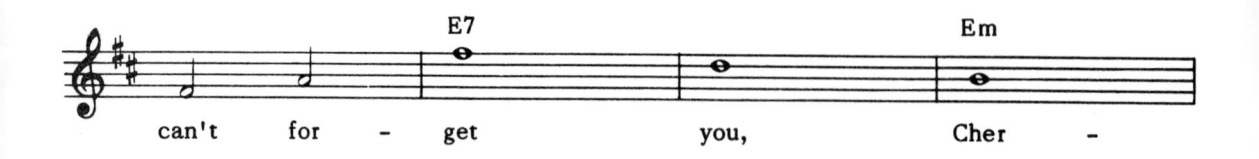

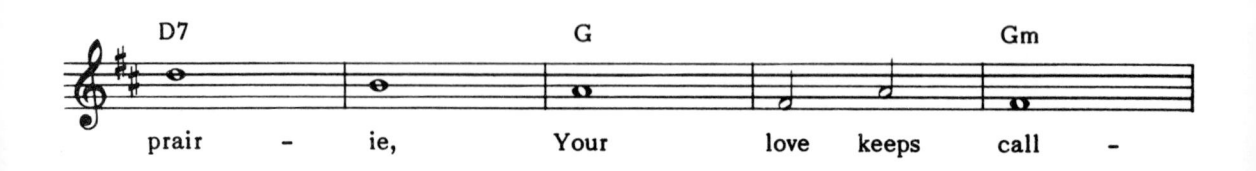

Words and Music by
RAY NOBLE

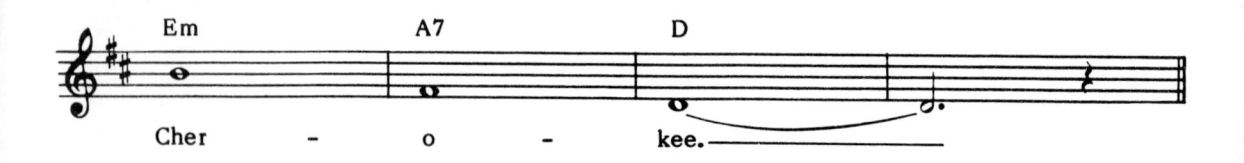

Moderately

Sweet Indian maiden, Since first I met you, I can't forget you, Cherokee, sweetheart. Child of the prairie, Your love keeps calling, My heart enthralling, Cherokee.

© 1938 & 1989 Peter Maurice & Co. Ltd., London WC2H 0EA

Dreams of summer time, Of lover time gone by. Throng my memory so tenderly and sigh. My sweet Indian maiden, One day I'll hold you, In my arms fold you, Cher-o-kee. kee.

CHICAGO

Words and Music by
FRED FISHER

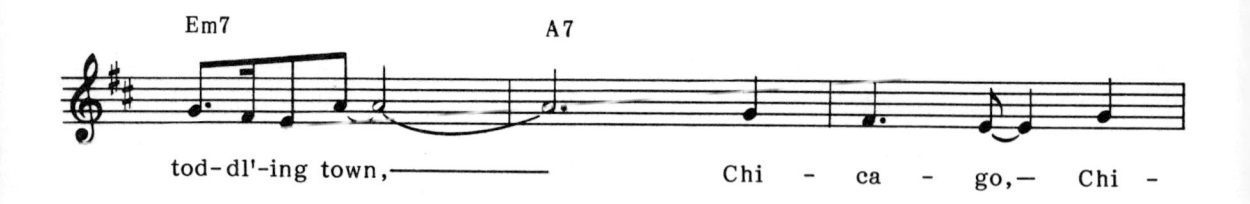

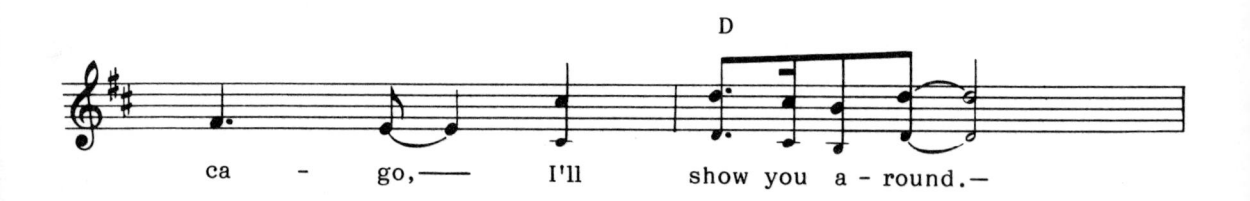

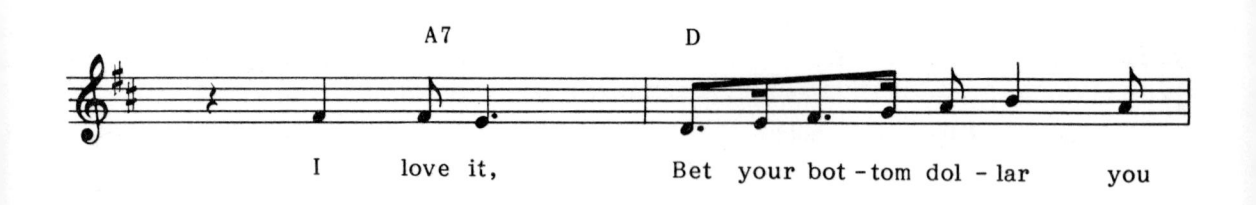

Brightly

Chi - ca - go,— Chi - ca - go,— That tod-dl'-ing town,——— Chi - ca - go,— Chi - ca - go,— I'll show you a - round.— I love it, Bet your bot-tom dol-lar you lose the blues— in Chi - ca - go,— Chi - ca - go,— The

© 1922 & 1989 Fred Fisher Music Co. Inc., USA
EMI Music Publishing Ltd., London WC2H 0EA

town that Billy Sunday could not shut down. Oh State Street, that great street, I just want to say They do things they don't do on Broadway, Say, They have the time, the time of their life, I saw a man, he danced with his wife, In Chicago, Chicago, my home town.

Chi-town.

CRAZY RHYTHM

Words by IRVING CAESAR
Music by JOSEPH MEYER and ROGER WOLFE KAHN

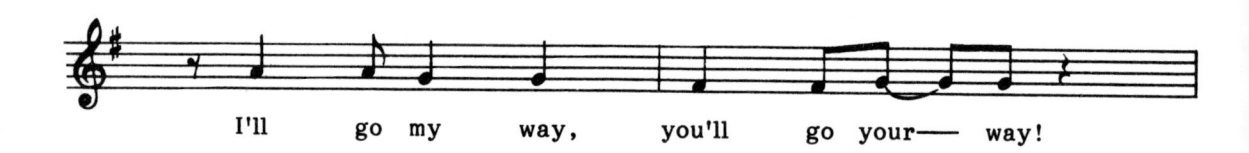

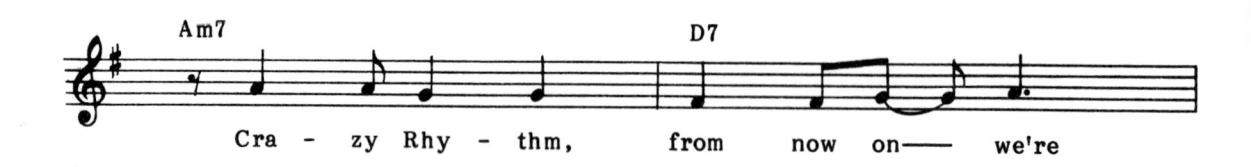

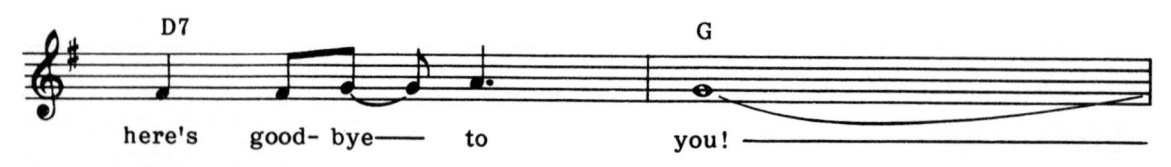

Not too fast

Cra - zy Rhy - thm, here's the door — way,

I'll go my way, you'll go your — way!

Cra - zy Rhy - thm, from now on — we're through. — Here is where we

have a show — down, I'm too high - hat,

you're too low — down. Cra - zy Rhy - thm,

here's good- bye — to you! —

© 1928 & 1989 Harms Inc., USA
Warner Chappell Music Ltd., Lodnon W1Y 3FA

They say that when a high-brow meets a low-brow Walking along Broadway, Soon the high-brow, he has no brow. Oh, it's a shame, and you're to balme. What's the use of Prohibition? You produce the same condition. Crazy Rhythm, I've gone crazy, too!

too!

THE DARKTOWN STRUTTERS' BALL

Words and Music by
SHELTON BROOKS

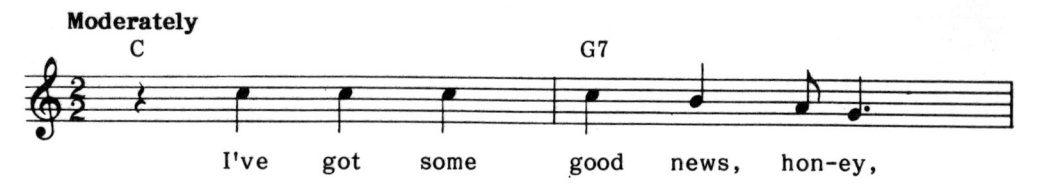

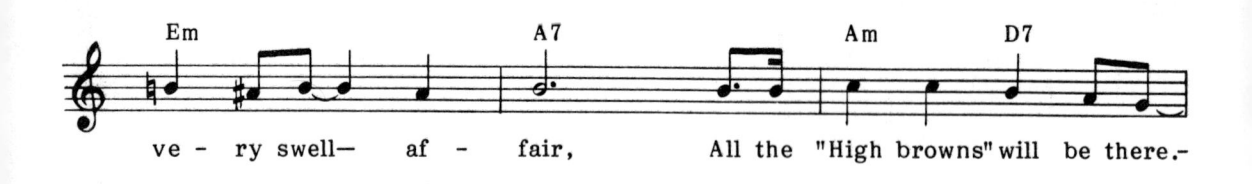

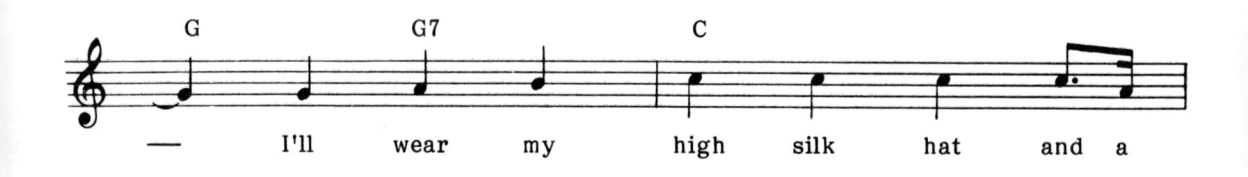

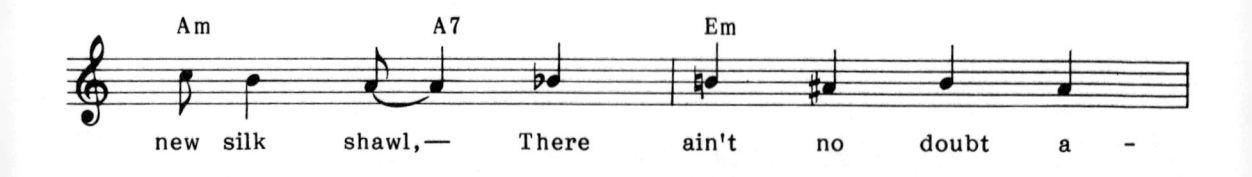

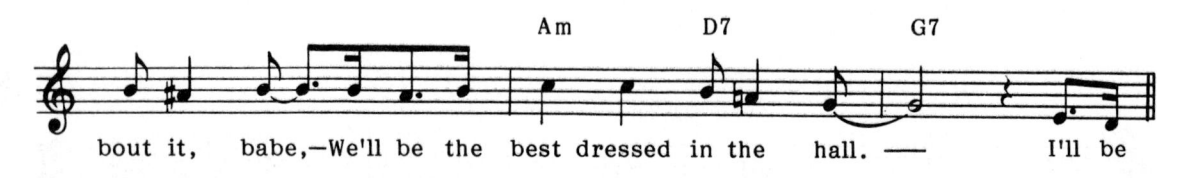

Moderately

I've got some good news, hon-ey, An in-vi-ta-tion to the Dark-town Ball, — It's a ve-ry swell— af-fair, All the "High browns" will be there.— I'll wear my high silk hat and a frock tail coat,— You wear your Par-is gown and your new silk shawl,— There ain't no doubt a-bout it, babe,—We'll be the best dressed in the hall. — I'll be

© 1917 & 1987 EMI Catalogue Partnership & EMI Feist Catalog Inc., USA
EMI United Partnership Ltd., London WC2H 0EA

Bright

down to get you in a taxi, honey, You better be ready about half past eight, Now dearie, don't be late, I want to be there when the band starts playing, Remember when we get there, honey, The two-steps, I'm goin' to have 'em all, Goin' to dance out both my shoes When they play the "Jelly Roll Blues," Tomorrow night at the Darktown Strutter's Ball.

1.
2. I'll be

HE'S GOT THE WHOLE WORLD IN HIS HANDS

Traditional

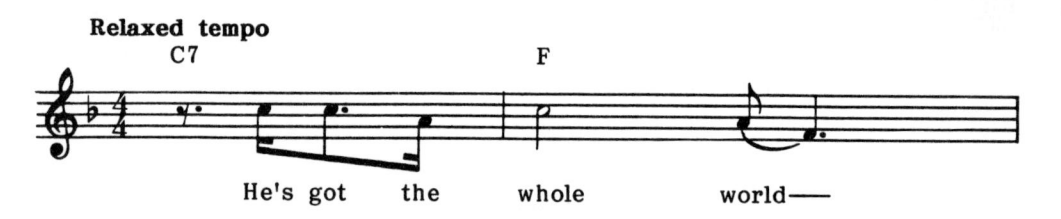

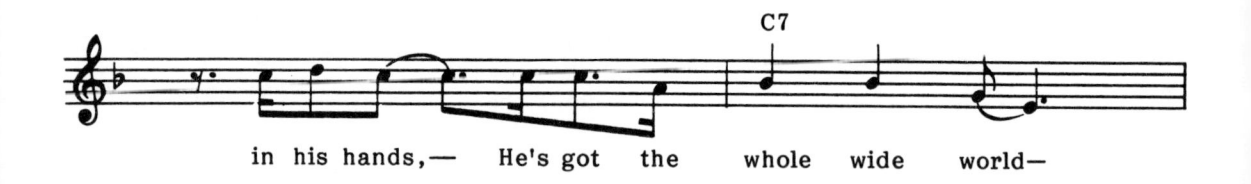

Relaxed tempo

He's got the whole world— in his hands,— He's got the whole wide world— in his hands;— He's got the whole world— in his hands,—He's got the whole world in his hands. He's got the lit-tle ti-ny ba-by in his hands,— He's got the

C7
lit - tle ti - ny ba - by in his hands;— He's got the

F
lit - tle ti - ny ba - by in his hands,— He's got the

C7	F	F
whole world in his hands. He's got the whole world—

	C7
in his hands,— He's got the whole wide world—

	F	
in his hands;—He's got the whole world— in his hands,—he's got the

C7	F
whole world in his hands.—————

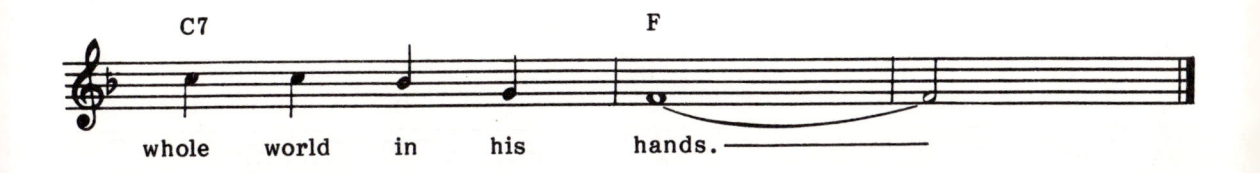

I GOT RHYTHM

Words and Music by
GEORGE and IRA GERSHWIN

Lively

Days can be sun-ny, With nev-er a sigh; Don't need what mon-ey can buy. Birds in the tree sing their day-ful of song, Why should-n't we sing a-long? I'm chip-per all the day, Hap-py with my lot. How do I get that way? Look at what I've got: I — got rhy-thm, — I — got mu-sic, — I — got my man, — Who could

© 1930 & 1989 New World Music Corp., USA
Warner Chappell Music Ltd., London W1Y 3FA

D7 G7 C C
ask for an-y-thing more? I —— got
Dm7 G7 C Dm7 G7
dais - ies— In —— green pas - tures,—
C Dm7 G7 D7 G7
I —— got my man,—Who could ask for an-y-thing
C E7
more? Old—— Man Trou - ble,—
A7 D7
I—— don't mind him,— You —— won't
G7
find him— 'Round—— my door.
C Dm7 G7 C
I —— got star - light,— I —— got
Dm7 G7 C Dm7 G7
sweet dreams,— I —— got my man,— Who could
C B♭ A7 D7 G7
ask for an- y-thing more, Who could ask for an-y-thing
1 C 2 C
more? —— more? ——

I'M GONNA SIT RIGHT DOWN AND WRITE MYSELF A LETTER

Words by JOE YOUNG
Music by FRED E AHLERT

Moderately

1. The mail man pass-es by And I just won-der why He nev-er stops to ring my front door bell.
2. Since you stopped writ-ing me I'm wor-ried as can be, I miss each lit-tle love word now and then.

There's not a sin-gle line From that dear old love of mine. No, not a word since I last heard "fare-well."

You're in my ev-'ry thought, You don't know how much I've fought To find a way to feel O. K. a-gain.

With a swing

I'm gon-na sit right down and write my-self a let-ter And make be-lieve it came from you.

© 1935 & 1989 Copyright renewed, reverted and assigned to Pencil Mark Music Inc., USA
Memory Lane Music Ltd/Anglo Pic Music Co. Ltd., London WC2H 8NA/Bucks Music Ltd., London W8 7SX

Dm		G7	

I'm gon-na write words, oh, so sweet, They're gon-na

C	A7	D7	

knock me off my feet. A lot of kiss-es on the

	G7		

bot-tom, I'll be glad I got 'em, I'm gon-na

C			

smile and say, "I hope you're feel-ing bet-ter"

	E7	F	A7

And close "with love" the way you do.

Dm	F	Fm	

I'm gon-na sit right down and write my-self a

C	A7	D7	G7

let-ter And make be-lieve it came from

1. C	G7	2. C	

you. I'm gon-na you.

IN THE MOOD

Words by ANDY RAZAF
Music by JOE GARLAND

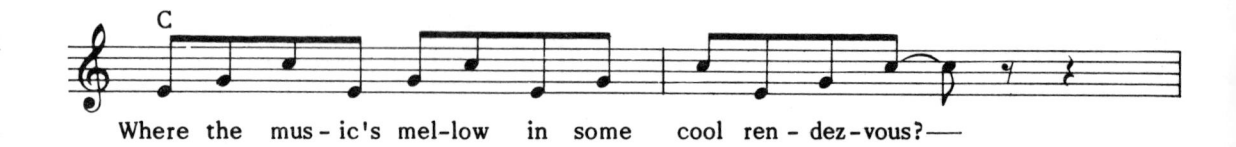

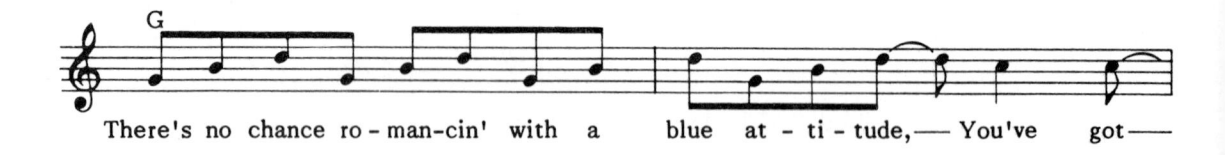

Bright

Mis-ter What-cha-call-um, what-cha do-in' to-night?—

Hope you're in the mood, be-cause I'm feel-in' just right.—

How's a-bout a cor-ner with a ta-ble for two—

Where the mus-ic's mel-low in some cool ren-dez-vous?—

There's no chance ro-man-cin' with a blue at-ti-tude,— You've got—

— to do some dancin' to get in the mood.— Sis-ter Whatchacallum, that's a

time-ly i-dea,— Some-thing swing-a-dil-la would be

good to my ear.— Ev-'ry-bo-dy must a-gree that

© 1939 & 1989 Shapiro Bernstein & Co. Inc., USA
Peter Maurice Music Co. Ltd., London WC2H 0EA

dan-cin' has charms— When you have that cer-tain one you love in your arms.— Step-pin' out with you will be a sweet in-ter-lude,— A build——er-up-per that will put me in the mood.— In the mood,— That's it, I've got it. In the mood,— Your ear will spot it. In the mood,— Oh, what a hot hit. Be a-live and get the jive, you've got to learn— how. Hep, hep hep,— Hep like a hep-per. Pep, pep pep,— Hot as a pep-per. Step, step step,— Step like a step-per. We're muggin' and hug-gin' we're in the mood—now. in the mood—now.

THE ENTERTAINER

by SCOTT JOPLIN

LIMEHOUSE BLUES

Words by DOUGLAS FURBER
Music by PHILIP BRAHM

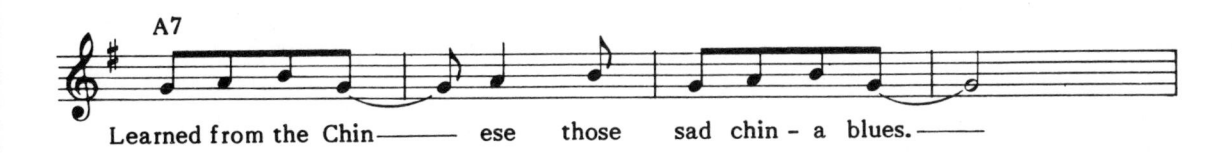

Moderately

[C7] Oh! Limehouse kid — Oh! Oh! Oh! Limehouse kid,

[A7] Going the way that the rest of them did.

[G] Poor Broken Blos — som and [B7] no - bo - dy's child, [Em]

[A7] Haunting and taunting you're just [D7] kind o' wild, — Oh! Oh!

[C7] Oh! Limehouse Blues — I've the real Limehouse Blues,

[A7] Learned from the Chin — ese those sad chin - a blues.

[G] Rings on your fin — gers and [E7] tears for your [Am] crown,

[D7] that is the sto — ry of [G] old Chin - a - town.

1. D.C. 2.

© 1922 & 1989 Ascherberg, Hopwood and Crew Ltd., London W1Y 3FA

SKYLINER

by CHARLIE BARNET

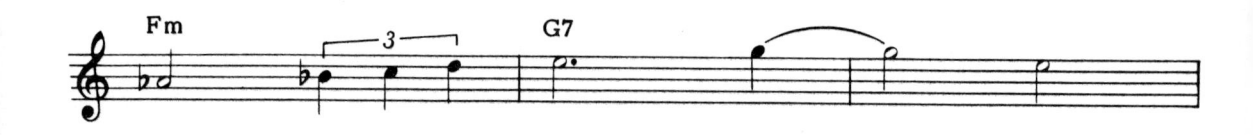

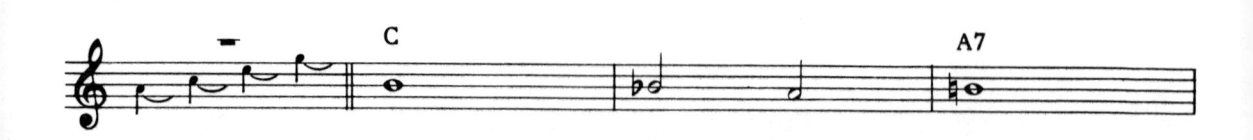

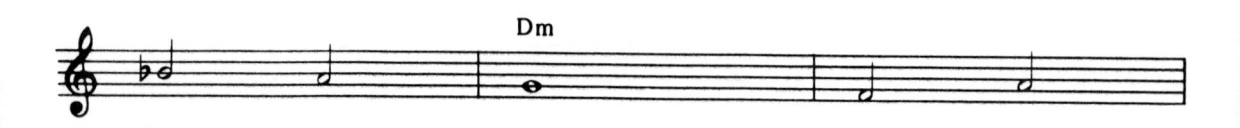

Slowly, not too fast

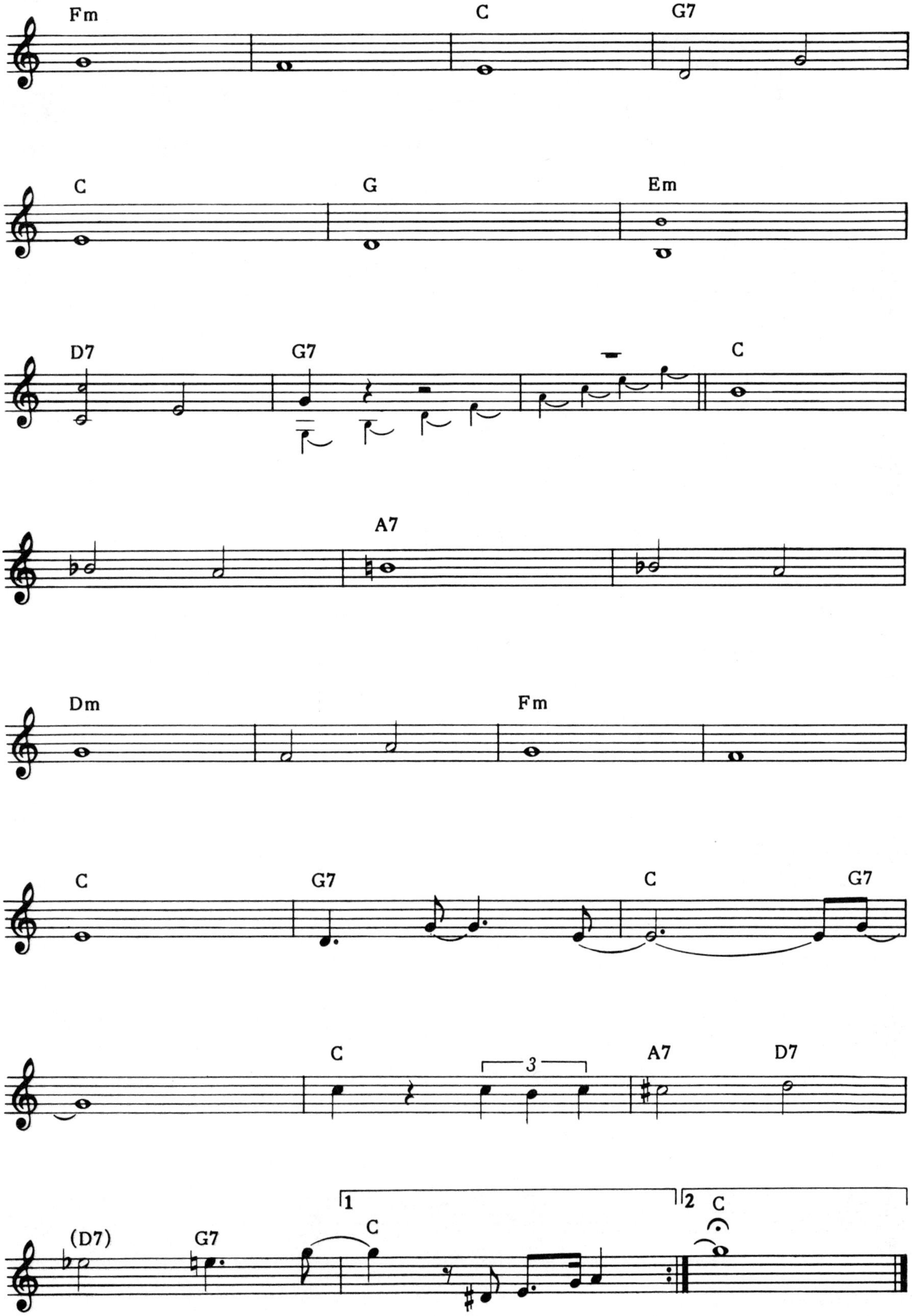
Fm
C
G7
C
G
Em
D7
G7
C
A7
Dm
Fm
C
G7
C
G7
C
3
A7
D7
(D7)
G7
1
C
2
C

SWEET GEORGIA BROWN

Words and Music by
MACEO PINKARD, KEN CASEY and BEN BERNIE

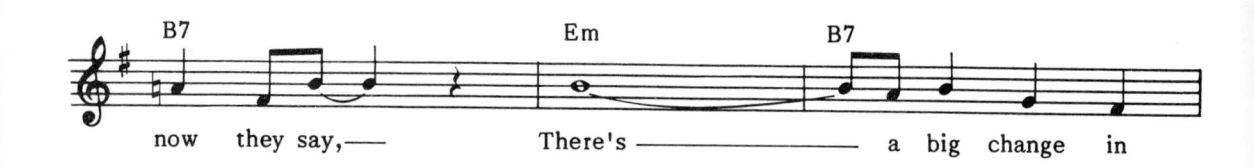

Moderately

1. She just got here yes-ter-day,— Things are hot here now they say,— There's———— a big change in town.———— Gals are jea-lous there's no doubt,— Still the fel-lows rave a-bout— Sweet,———— sweet Georgia Brown.———— And ev-er since she came— You'll hear the folks all claim, say,

With a swing

No gal made— has got the shade— On sweet Geor-gia Brown,—

© 1925 & 1989 Remick Music Corp., USA
Francis Day & Hunter Ltd., London WC2H 0EA/Redwood Music Ltd., London NW1 8BD

Two left feet, but, oh! so neat has sweet Georgia Brown. They all sigh and wanna die For sweet Georgia Brown, I'll tell you just why. You know I don't lie, Not much. It's been said she knocks 'em dead when she lands in town. Since she came, why it's a shame how she cools 'em down. Fell-ers she can't get are fell-ers she ain't met, Georgia claimed her, Georgia named her Sweet Georgia Brown.

TIGER RAG (HOLD THAT TIGER!)

Words by HARRY DeCOSTA
Music by ORIGINAL DIXIELAND JAZZ BAND

Fast

Where's that ti-ger?— Can't find that ti-ger.— Lost that ti-ger,— Ain't seen that ti-ger.— Where's that ti-ger?— Hold that ti-ger.— Lost that ti-ger,— Has an-y-bo-dy seen that ti-ger?

Instrumental

Hold that ti-ger, Hold that ti-ger, Hold that

© 1917, 1932 & 1989 EMI Catalogue Partnership and EMI Feist Catalog Inc., USA
EMI United Partnership Ltd., London WC2H 0EA

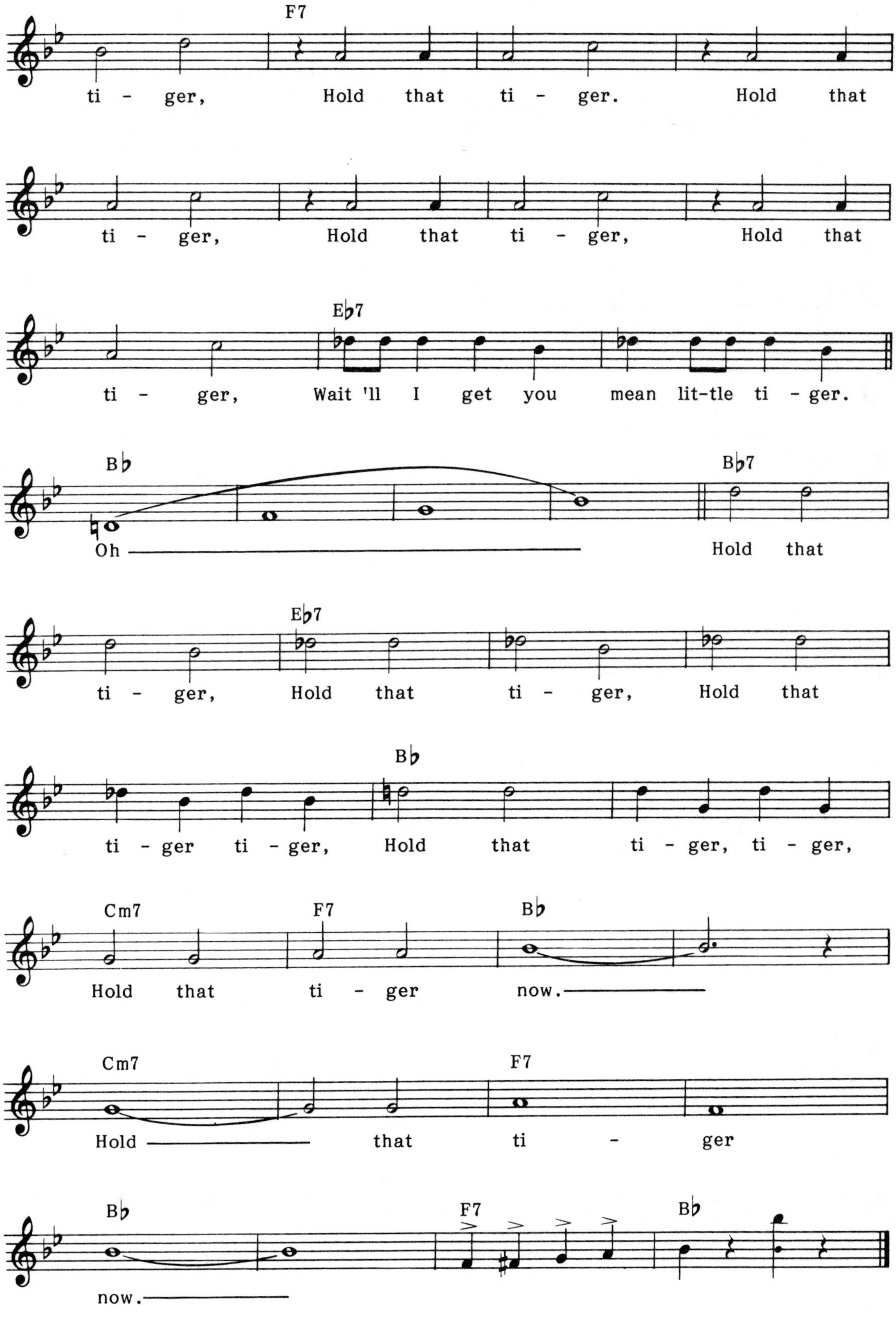
F7
ti - ger, Hold that ti - ger. Hold that
ti - ger, Hold that ti - ger, Hold that
E♭7
ti - ger, Wait 'll I get you mean lit-tle ti - ger.
B♭
B♭7
Oh Hold that
E♭7
ti - ger, Hold that ti - ger, Hold that
B♭
ti - ger ti - ger, Hold that ti - ger, ti - ger,
Cm7
F7
B♭
Hold that ti - ger now.
Cm7
F7
Hold that ti - ger
B♭
F7
B♭
now.

12TH STREET RAG

Words by ANDY RAZAF
Music by EUDAY L BOWMAN

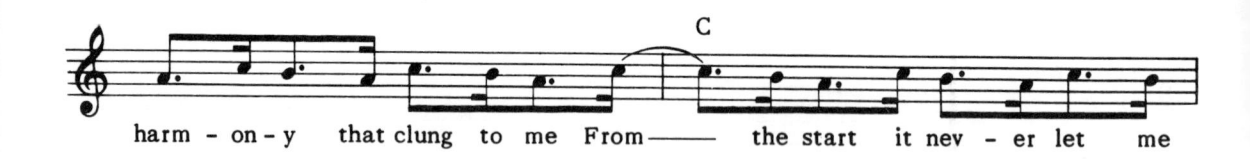

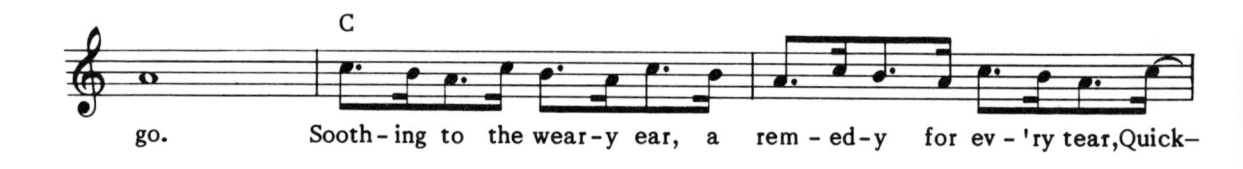

Moderately

Down in Kan-sas Ci-ty some-one wrote a pret-ty dit-ty, A mel-o-dy for all the world to know, Full of cling-y, swing-y, sing-y harm-on-y that clung to me From the start it nev-er let me go. Sooth-ing to the wear-y ear, a rem-ed-y for ev-'ry tear, Quick-to put some gin-ger in your feet. Some treat, sweet heat, That's the tune that they call "12th Street." Joy to each ro-man-cer and de-light of ev-'ry dan-cer And luck—

© 1914 & 1989 Euday L Bowman, USA
Copyright renewed 1941 Euday L Bowman
© 1942 Shapiro, Bernstein & Co. Inc., USA
Warner Chappell Music Ltd., London W1Y 3FA

—y to the lead-er of a band, In a ball-room or a show and o-ver an-y rad-i-o, Bet— your boots that it will get a hand. You can brag, it's in the bag When they play that 12th Street Rag.—

Oh! 12th— Street Rag, have pit-y. Won't you let— me be? Go back— to Kan-sas Ci—ty And stop trail—ing me. You barge— in at the moment When I've work to do. I can't shake you, You won't leave and I can't make you. Ole music man who wrote you knew no sympathy. I hope you get his goat, too Like you worry me. I'm swing bent, my brain is 'sent' on a jag When I hear that 12th Street Rag.

WHEN THE SAINTS GO MARCHING IN

43

Traditional

Brightly

1. Oh, when the saints — Go march-ing in, —
   crown — him Lord of All, —
   Oh, when the saints go march - ing in, —
   Oh, when they crown him Lord of All, —
   Dear Lord, I want to be in that num - ber, —
   Dear Lord, I want to be in that num - ber, —
   When the saints go march - ing in. — 2. Oh, when the
   When they crown him Lord of All. — 4. Oh, when they
   sun — re - fuse to shine, — Oh, when the
   gath — er 'round the throne, — Oh, when they
   sun re - fuse to shine, — Dear Lord, I
   gath - er 'round the throne, — Dear Lord, I
   want to be in that num - ber, — When the
   want to be in that num - ber, — When they
   sun re - fuse to shine. — 3. Oh, when they
   gath - er 'round the throne.

© 1989 International Music Publications Limited, Woodford Green, Essex IG8 8HN

Reproduced and printed by
Halstan & Co. Ltd., Amersham, Bucks., England